STREAMER-FLY FISHING

Books by John Merwin

Fly Fishing: A Trailside Guide
Well-Cast Lines
The New American Trout Fishing
The Battenkill
John Merwin's Fly-Tying Guide
The Freshwater Tacklebox
The Saltwater Tacklebox
Stillwater Trout

STREAMER-FLY FISHING

John Merwin

THE LYONS PRESS

Printed in Canada

10   9   8   7   6   5   4   3   2

Library of Congress Cataloging-in-Publication Data

Merwin, John.
    Streamer-fly fishing / John Merwin.
        p.   cm.
    ISBN 1-58574-041-1
    1. Fly fishing.   I. Title
SH456.M46 1991
799.1'2—dc20   90-23172
                                                    CIP

Contents

Introduction

Z onker. Now there's a name. It's anything but subtle and carries all the pop-culture clout of a Roy Lichtenstein painting in the exaggerated comic-book style of POP! POW! BAM! and ZOWIE! It happens to be a streamer fly, and so it is with streamers.

These are flies of a robust honesty. Joe's Smelt is a streamer that sounds incapable of deceit, other than the honorable one of fooling trout. Like Joe, it's a regular fly. Thus Chief Needahbeh sports bright red-and-yellow feathers over his long-shanked hook. Thus a Gray Ghost slips along quietly over a shoal of smelt, and a Muddler putt-putts and muddles across a Rocky Mountain river.

A Red Quill dry fly, I submit, neither reds nor quills. A nymph doesn't nymph, and a Royal Coachman wet neither royals nor coaches. Streamers are the active flies. Flies with muscle in their names. Flies that catch big fish. A happy bit of vaudeville livening up fly boxes that grow increasingly dull with every modern season.

This book is about catching trout with streamers and bucktails. These are imitations of small fish that big fish eat, and so streamers are big-fish flies. Bucktails are those minnow imitations with hair-wings; streamers are those with feather wings. Wings of mixed materials have become commonplace, so I sometimes use "streamers" and "bucktails" interchangeably and more often just "streamers" to mean the entire range of such flies.

Of all the flies available to modern trout fishermen, streamers are the least popular in terms of sales. They require the most work from an angler to fish well, which is probably the reason for lower sales. The classic and colorful combinations of floss, feather, and fur that came out of the Maine woods between the world wars are disappearing from many fly shops, too, because the art of their tying is beyond most large-scale commercial tying houses. There is a growing trend toward only a few patterns in most boxes—a Blacknose Dace, perhaps, plus some more modern Zonkers, Buggers, and Muddlers—of which any fly fisherman can make good use anywhere.

Streamer flies are widely used in fresh and salt water for fish other than trout, of course. It's hard to find a fish species that *won't* take streamers. This book's length was defined before it was written and is barely long enough to deal with trout, so that's where we stop.

You needn't stop there, however, and your next step should be to read *Streamers and Bucktails,* by the late Joseph D. Bates. Joe, whom I knew well, took his book through several editions, starting in 1950 with *Streamer-Fly Fishing.* He corresponded with fly tiers and fishermen from all over the world for more than fifty years, and from all those letters and fly samples grew his books.

Some History and Theory

Streamers and bucktails didn't come into widespread and deliberate use as minnow imitations until after the First World War—several centuries after other wet flies became commonplace. Making artificial minnows out of feathers and fur is such a simple idea that many writers have wondered in print why it took such a long time to develop.

The answer is relatively simple and depends largely on attitudes toward fishing that prevailed in general during the eighteenth and nineteenth centuries both in America and Great Britain. Historical angling practice is part of the answer, too, as is the reason fly fishing developed in the first place. Here's a clue: Real minnows are fairly tough and work well as a natural bait. The insects upon which trout also feed are fragile and difficult to use as bait.

Because natural insects are fragile, it's easier and more effective to use an imitation. My intuition tells me artificial flies thus came about as a practical matter and not from a higher sense of sportsmanship, which came later. Minnow imitations were another matter. Since it was perfectly easy and effective to use the natural bait, there was less need for an imitation. I've had the opportunity to examine many old fly wallets—most from after the Civil War, but a few dating back almost to 1800—and commonly in such collections are numerous wet flies, perhaps a few salmon wet flies, plus an assortment of other items, including "minnow tackle." Such tackle was often a pair of naked hooks snelled one behind the other on a gut leader, which allowed a ready strike when a trout came to the attached minnow teased across the current.

This was back when the term "fly" meant insect imitations; an artificial anything-else was a lure. This distinction is still maintained in

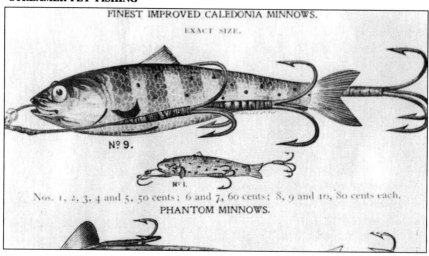

FINEST IMPROVED CALEDONIA MINNOWS.

EXACT SIZE.

Nº 9.

Nº 1.

Nos. 1, 2, 3, 4 and 5, 50 cents; 6 and 7, 60 cents; 8, 9 and 10, 80 cents each.

PHANTOM MINNOWS.

Imitation minnow from a circa 1890 Orvis catalog. Bare-hook gangs for fishing real minnows were made in similar fashion.

Great Britain, where our modern streamer flies are often called lures. Thus semantically, and from a practical angling view as well, the concept of streamer flies was far removed from fly fishing through most of its history.

There is not much difference, of course, between a small streamer fly and a large wet fly, and there's little doubt that some of the trout caught one or two centuries ago were striking at flies that looked and behaved like minnows. That seems to have been an imitative accident, however, and our real streamers and bucktails didn't come about until almost 1900.

By this time, Americans were fly fishing on both coasts and just about everywhere in between. Metropolitan sportsmen were starting to travel widely. A number of fishing mail-order businesses were well established, and there were numerous periodicals devoted wholly or in part to angling and featuring a variety of debates in their letters columns that included vigorous arguments as to the relative merits of the then newly introduced brown trout. Saltwater fly fishing was a new and growing sport, and fly fishing for freshwater bass was also becoming more popular. Streamers and bucktails for trout were part of this

4

growth, but their parentage is uncertain. In fact, there probably wasn't a specific parent at all.

Various people—including Theodore Gordon, Alonzo Bacon, Herbert Welch, Emerson Hough, and William Scripture—have taken or been given credit for developing streamers around this time. Their respective work took place within a span of a few years and apparently independently. New ideas in angling traveled much more widely and quickly now than they did before the Civil War, and minnow imitations were soon part of every man's angling arsenal. Even then, however, these new flies didn't eclipse more traditional wet-fly patterns except in one area: southwestern Maine.

In the greater Rangeley region of Maine, brook trout were growing to ten pounds and even larger feeding on smaller blueback trout and smelt. The same was true of landlocked salmon, although its original distribution in Maine (and elsewhere) was much more limited than that of the common brookie. It was (and is) a fishery tailor-made for streamer flies, and it was here that our most elegant patterns were developed. Long and slim fly profiles matched the smelt's shape, and

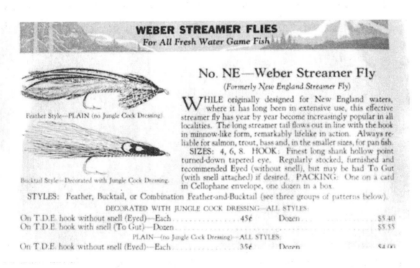

Weber in Stevens Point, Wisconsin, was a major fly-manufacturing company before the Second World War. This illustration is from a 1938 Weber catalog, which was one of the first to feature a wide selection of streamer flies.

5

Maine brook trout and landlocked salmon feed largely on smelt, which led to the development of numerous well-known streamer patterns. This Maine landlock took a Supervisor streamer while actively feeding on smelt.

colors both muted and brilliant marked different fly patterns developed to accommodate whimsy on the part of both fishermen and fish.

Those trout are much smaller now, and the little bluebacks on which they fed are extinct in all but a few smaller ponds. The fly patterns endured, however, brought back to New York and Boston by the many sportsmen who frequented Rangeley between the wars, and from there taken North, South, and West both in fly boxes and in print. Gray Ghosts, Black Ghosts, Supervisors, Edson Tigers, and the rest are still common currency in much of the country, and the ideas they represent gave rise to most of the more modern patterns also discussed in this book.

Streamer flies work because big fish eat little fish. This is a simple idea only until it's explored. Young trout start out by eating zooplankton and insect larvae in proportion to their small size. Soon the trout graduate to feeding on what's called *drift*, meaning those insect larvae and adults brought to the trout's feeding station by the current. At a point that varies with such things as habitat, available food, and fish species, the fish become more and more piscivorous (fish-eating), and less and less dependent on insect fare. With brown trout, this often starts to happen when the fish reaches ten or twelve inches. This change in diet means the trout can continue to get bigger, and the largest trout often eat almost nothing but other fish.

To a certain extent, different kinds of trout show this tendency toward dietary changes differently. Both brown and brook trout tend heavily to a diet of other fish as they grow, but this is somewhat less true of rainbow trout, for example. Brook trout were originally an eastern species, and rainbow trout were once native only to the Pacific Coast. At the same time that streamer patterns were being developed for brookies in the Northeast, anglers like Roderick Haig-Brown, Tommy Brayshaw, and Bill Nation were experimenting with *insect-imitating* wet and dry flies for rainbows in the far Northwest. There

The other "big-fish" photos in this book notwithstanding, this small brown trout represents an average catch almost anywhere in America. At this size, browns will start to switch from eating insects to eating small fish, which enables them to grow much larger.

were a very few northwestern streamer patterns in the 1930s, to be sure, but the emphasis was far different. The northwestern tradition of trout and steelhead involves just about every kind of fly *except* streamers, and I hope by so stating to have written myself out of any accusations of geographical bias.

It's worth noting that this change from an insect- to a fish-based diet may vary dramatically among individual fish of the same species in the same stream. Thus, a brown trout that never switches may die of old age after seven years and at thirteen inches. In the next pool, another brown trout may be more than twenty-four inches long and weigh five pounds or more at the same age simply because the second individual switched from insects to fish in its adolescence. From a behavioral and evolutionary view, the latter fish is more successful, and it is on that success that streamer fishing is based.

Most streamer flies look like prey species of one sort or another. If the fly behaves in that fashion near a trout, most of the time the trout will try to eat it and be caught. Thus, given the right fly, which is no small matter, successful streamer fishing is a matter of making your fly behave in a lifelike manner. Sometimes this is easily done, but the exceptions—and there are many—make the sport. We'll explore many of those in the following chapters.

Tackle

2

Y ou can fish streamer flies for trout with any sort of fly tackle you happen to have. But the more you fish, the more you'll encounter some special tackle needs for streamer fishing. We'll explore some of those needs in this chapter, where you'll find that solving the problems of streamer tackle for trout can also set you up quite well for some types of salmon, steelhead, bass, and light-tackle saltwater fishing. There's thus some economy in accommodating the special needs of this particular trout-fishing method.

As with many other sorts of fly fishing, streamer-fly tackle is dictated most by the size of the flies you'll be casting. Simply put, big flies such as are commonly used on big rivers require a heavy-line rod for adequate casting. Conversely, those anglers using small streamers and bucktails in little creeks and brooks can use comparably lighter tackle.

Streamer-fly fishing, more than other type of fly fishing, may require wider use of the full range of fly-line types available from major manufacturers. Although the brook fisherman may only need a floating line, moving to a bigger river can require the use of sinking lines of assorted densities. On some rivers I've switched among four different lines for the same rod in one day's fishing to get the fly near the fish successfully.

Rods

Being able to manipulate and control your fly line on the water after you cast is the key to successful streamer fishing, and a longer rod makes this task much easier. Rods of nine or nine and a half feet are thus more effective tools than the shorter rods with which beginning trout fishermen commonly start.

Smaller streams can be streamer-fished with light-line rods, but you'll still need a long rod for adequate line control.

Older fly-fishing books described streamer rods of split bamboo as long, heavy-line rods with a slow action. The Orvis Battenkills and heavier Paul Young Parabolic models are a couple of examples, the former having been a favorite of the late Joe Brooks, who did much to popularize streamer fishing from the 1950s through the early 1970s. One of Brooks's pet streamer rods was an eight-and-a-half-foot Battenkill for an 8-weight line, which I also owned and fished for a number of years. The deep, powerful flex of this rod helped me to throw a big Muddler for a remarkable distance over big water. Its action was so slow that I often felt as if I had time for a sip of coffee while waiting for the cast to straighten over a deep and distant riffle.

The rod was also heavy and exhausting to cast for any length of time. After an hour or so my forearm muscles started to cramp, and I spent more time than I'd have liked resting the water and my arm. The rod, I decided, had been built back when men were men and was no tool for a pencil-pushing desk jockey like me. So I sold the rod and made the happy switch to graphite.

The advent of graphite as fly-rod material in 1973 revolutionized all of fly fishing. Light in weight and stiffer than bamboo, graphite rods allowed casters to develop higher line speeds and thus to cast farther. Most pertinent to streamer fishing, powerful rods could be built both long and light, desirable characteristics that are mutually exclusive in describing bamboo. One of my new favorite streamer rods—a two-piece, nine-foot graphite for a 7-weight line—weighs in at a mere three ounces, which is less than half the weight of a comparable bamboo model.

Like bamboo, graphite rods are available in a variety of actions. I've encountered graphite rods that were so stiff—fast-actioned—as to be unpleasant in casting, and a very few others that were so soft—

Really big water such as this often demands big flies or heavy shooting heads, and you'll want a 9-weight outfit or even heavier in a length of nine-feet or even longer.

Somewhat larger rivers often mean larger flies and call for lines in the 6- or 7-weight range. A 9 foot rod is probably the ideal streamer-fishing length.

slow-actioned—as to be almost useless. Both extremes are exceptions, however, and within the range of commonly available graphite rods it's now difficult to find a bad one.

Graphite rods with a relatively easy progressive action are the easiest to cast, especially with large streamer flies that tend to be heavy and sometimes air-resistant. Historically, rod makers have never been able to agree on or to standardize terms that characterize rod actions, a situation as true in this age of graphite as it was 100 years ago in the early days of bamboo.

Rod makers now are using graphite fibers of varying *modulus,* which is a physical constant that describes the fiber's relative stiffness in millions of pounds per square inch (modulus of elasticity). I've looked at the formula by which this constant is calculated and decided it was sufficiently complicated to be off limits for any fishing book. What you might want to remember as you compare the modulus figures given by various makers is that the relationship of one modulus figure to another is linear. That is, a fiber with a modulus of 40 million is twice as stiff as one with a modulus of 20 million.

This doesn't mean that one rod will be twice as stiff as another, however, and that's the rub for the streamer fisherman searching for a rod. Rod action is as much determined by the maker's taper design as it is by the material used. It's entirely possible, for example, to make a slow-actioned rod from a high-modulus fiber.

What may help you to choose among the hundreds of graphite rod models now available is some knowledge of design trends. High-modulus graphite fiber (48-million-plus) has been all the rage for the past couple of years among major rod makers. Almost all of these rods have been designed with very fast actions that offer an edge only to very experienced casters. Older designs, and those typically based on lower-modulus fibers, are usually of a slower action and I prefer them for that reason. They are simply easier to cast. Happily, and with a few significant exceptions, lower-priced graphite rods—in the $75 to $250 range—are typically of a slower action than are those rods costing significantly more.

There is one limited area of streamer-fly tactics in which all major rod makers are sadly lacking, and that's in long single-handed rods for ultra-heavy lines. Virtually all graphite rods for line weights 10 and higher are extremely stiff and uncomfortable to cast. These are the so-called tarpon rods built to handle an occasional cast but with more emphasis on stiffness and fish-fighting power. There are rare times when I want to throw a huge hair sucker or big wool sculpin (by big I mean about six inches long) on a heavy shooting head in big water. I've asked most of the major makers in person for a heavy-line easy-casting rod, and most have acknowledged they simply don't build one. The closest rod I've found is one nine-and-a-half-foot 10-weight, and I'm still looking.

For the time being, let's standardize our streamer rod as a nine-foot graphite model with a moderate action. The most widely useful line weight is a 7, so a nine-foot 7-weight model is *the* all-around streamer rod. I've used this rod with streamers for everything from big Labrador brook trout to big rainbows in California's Fall River and on to Alaska with numerous stops in between. This rod has also doubled for light-tackle salmon and steelhead fishing, bass-bugging with smaller bass flies, and even bonefish if there's no wind—it's a good investment.

For some streamer fishing, however, this rod will be too heavy or too light. Once again, brook fishermen will want a smaller line for small streamers, and a 7-weight is itself too light for heaving a shooting head across the wide Missouri. Here's a chart that correlates fly size, river examples, and line weights that can help you choose a nine-foot rod of appropriate line size.

Maximum Fly Size	Line Weights	River Examples
# 10	2, 3, and 4	Small brooks and creeks
# 6	5 and 6	Small to medium-size rivers
# 1/0	7 and 8	Medium to large rivers
# 3/0+	9+	Very large rivers

This is arbitrary to an extent, but it's difficult if not dangerous to cast a 1/0 streamer with a 4-weight rod, and fishing midget bucktails with an 8-weight usually means you're overgunned. I've also used 8- and 9-weight outfits to plumb the depths of relatively small rivers, and have occasionally used lighter outfits on bigger water. Use the chart as a guide to the streamer fishing you do *most* of the time.

Reels

Streamers are often used in anticipation of big fish, so make sure your reel is up to the task. You may fish small Squirrel Tails over little stocked browns in a suburban stream for years and never use your reel as a fish-fighting tool. But when that once-in-a-lifetime five-pounder whacks your bucktail and runs out of the pool, your neglected reel might cost you the fish.

The majority of fly reels have a simple click-drag system. If yours is adjustable, keep it set fairly light with just enough tension to keep the spool from overrunning and tangling when you give a sharp yank on the line. Make sure, also, that your reel will carry at least 100 yards of *thirty-pound test* braided Dacron backing. I use close to 200 yards on almost all of my reels as a matter of course. Most manufacturers stipulate twenty-pound test backing, but the larger diameter of the heavier backing is much less prone to tangles and jamming on the spool.

I have caught trout well over ten pounds—plus large Atlantic salmon and steelhead—on simple click-drag reels, but in every case I've wished for something better. Dedicated streamer fishermen are deliberately gunning for big fish, and something better in the reel department is usually appropriate. "Better" in this case means with a more sophisticated drag system.

Drag systems on most modern fly reels fall in two categories: those with caliper systems like disc brakes on a car, and those that depend on the friction produced by compressed drag washers of metal, cork, and/or Teflon. I have had no bad experiences with either type. Such reels used to be horribly expensive, and some still are, albeit lovely tools to be treasured for a lifetime. There are now several reel models with these features, however, that retail for less than $100 with comparably inexpensive spare spools.

Whatever drag system you use, make sure it works smoothly *before* you go fishing. After the reel has been spooled with line, adjust the drag so that when you hold the reel suspended by the line the reel descends slowly and smoothly to the floor. If the descent is halting or jerky, your drag needs work. Take the reel apart (or go back to the dealer and have him do this) and polish only the metal-bearing surfaces of either the drag washers or the metal disc rotor. Leave the soft washers and/or the disc-bearing pads alone. The object is to make the metal-bearing surfaces perfectly flat, so rub the washers on a flat

15

oilstone or on fine emery paper placed on a flat surface. Any high spots on the drag washers will be quickly evident and must be smoothed out so that the metal-bearing surface is flat and ultra-smooth. Clean the metal parts and reassemble the drag components *without* any oil or grease unless specifically called for by the manufacturer. Oil and grease will usually cause dirt retention in the drag system and ruin all your work. The soft drag washers and/or brake pads are usually self-lubricating, anyway. After you've finished, store your reel with the drag adjustment backed all the way off to avoid permanent deformation of the soft drag washers and/or brake pads.

Most fly fisherman, having acquired a wonderful new adjustable-drag reel, use a drag setting that's much too heavy. This just invites hook pull-outs, broken tackle, and lost fish. The advantage of an adjustable drag is smoothness and adjustability over a range of light settings, and not that it allows one to screw down the washers and horse big fish. Most big trout, with the exception of some big brookies, will make a strong run when first hooked, and you want a drag setting that will let the fish run relatively freely—tiring itself in that first explosive effort so you can get down to the real fight. Trying to stop such a fish initially with a heavy drag means that first burst of energy will go into head-shaking and a vicious rolling that will almost certainly cause the hook to pull out or the tippet or knot to fail. As with a click-drag reel, use a drag setting just heavy enough to keep the spool from overrunning, and apply additional pressure as needed by braking the spool with your fingertips or squeezing the line between the rod grip and your hand throughout the fight. Don't monkey with the drag setting while you're fighting a fish. It's too easy to make a mistake.

Lines

Fly lines have become increasingly varied and specialized in recent years, giving a streamer fisher greater latitude than ever. You can buy a line specifically for delicacy or for distance. You can also buy lines that float, sink, or do both, which allow you to fish on top or at any depth in any sort of current short of a waterfall.

A weight-forward floating line is an obvious first choice and maximizes both distance and your ability to control a cast once it's on the water. Some modern designs feature harder exterior finishes and/or stiffer cores, which reduce tangles and add distance to your casts.

Your second line should be a sinker, and here the choices are much wider. Sinking lines now have various sink rates, which are usually specified in inches per second. This designation is a significant and recent advance that allows you to compare apples to apples among sinking lines. There are also full-sinking lines (the whole line sinks) and sinking-tip lines (in which the forward portion sinks and the rear portion floats). This means you can mend the floating portion on the water and better control the drift of the sinking front end. Sinking-tip lines are available in assorted sink rates and typically with either a short sinking tip (ten feet or so) or a long sinking tip that may be twenty feet or even longer. I'll describe the setups I use with these lines, which aren't the only choices but may help you get started.

For a typical day on a fast-flowing trout stream anywhere in the country I use one rod, two reels, and plan on fishing streamers part of the time. The size of the rod and reel/line combinations is scaled to my fly size, the size of the water I'm fishing, and the size of the biggest fish I hope to encounter.

One reel is set up with a weight-forward floating line that I'll use for streamers and other sorts of fly fishing. The other reel is set up with a sinking-tip line in which the sinking portion is very fast sinking, which I've found to be the most useful in general streamer fishing. Since I'm typically drifting a streamer through a riffle and into a deep hole, I want the fly to get down *fast* and stay there. All sinking lines are buoyed upward by the current, and fast sinkers fish deeper in moving water. If it's big water, like New Hampshire's Androscoggin, Montana's Madison, or California's Pit River, I'll likely have a long sinking tip. For smaller or more gently flowing rivers, I'll use a short one. (I use two reels, by the way, since I've found it easier than fumbling around trying to change spools. Suit yourself.)

Another option is a series of shooting-taper lines, which is what I use if I expect to be streamer-fishing only on moderate- to large-size rivers. Repetitive distance casting—a cornerstone of streamer fishing—is easiest with a shooting taper, and I can also fish a sinking shooting head more deeply than any other sort of line if need be. The terms "shooting taper" and "shooting head" are synonymous, by the way. Shooting Head, however, is a trademark of the old Sunset Line

This big sea-run rainbow took a large orange-marabou streamer fished on a lead-core shooting head backed by monofilament running line for maximum fishing depth.

Company in California and other manufacturers had to develop another term to describe the same thing. Shooting head has been commonly accepted in the fly fisher's vocabulary, and that's the term I'll use henceforth.

In fishing with shooting heads, my reel is set up with about 100 feet of running line ahead of the backing. This may be small-diameter floating fly line, sold especially for use with shooting heads, if I don't expect to be fishing at maximum depths. For fishing really deep fast-flowing water I use monofilament running line. It's generally smaller in diameter than floating running line, which means less water resistance and deeper fishing with a fast-sinking shooting head.

I usually carry four or five different shooting heads of different sink rates, each one fastened in coiled fashion with pipe cleaners and stored in a zip-lock bag that I've labeled as to the head's size and sink rate. Each head has a leader butt permanently affixed to one end with a nail knot and a loop on the other end for attaching the running line. I clinch-knot the running line to this loop when I change heads, which

The author with a brook trout in far northern Quebec, where these wilderness fish proved exceptionally selective as to streamer pattern and color.

I think is simpler than the loop-to-loop connection some people use.

Streamer fishing can involve big flies and big water, and a shooting-head system is by far the easiest method of fly fishing in this case. I can alter my fishing depth easily by changing heads, and repetitive long-distance casting is much easier with a shooting head than with other types of lines. With shooting heads, however, I don't have the precision of line and fly control that I have with full fly lines, which is why I don't use shooting heads all the time.

Leaders

It's now simplest to buy tailor-made leaders with suitable butt and tippet dimensions calibrated to your line and fly sizes. In general, streamer flies are heavy, especially when wet, and a stiff-butted leader will produce a better turnover on the cast. The braided-butt leaders that some now prefer for fishing with smaller flies are not good streamer leaders. For streamer fishing with a floating line, a knotless tapered leader nine feet long should be perfectly adequate as long as the butt diameter is .021 inches or greater and the tippet is sufficiently heavy for the flies you're fishing. I rarely use anything smaller than 3X, even with small streamers, and often use 0X or even heavier with larger flies. If the leader isn't turning over properly on your cast, use a smaller fly or cut back the tippet to a heavier section.

With sinking lines, your leader should be substantially shorter. I don't like weighted streamers. The weight detracts from the fly's action in the water. A long leader with an unweighted fly will be buoyed upward by the current, even as the sinking line sinks, and is self-defeating. So I use a leader butt about eighteen inches long and an interlocking loop connection to attach another eighteen inches of tippet material. I use double surgeon's knots to make the loops.

Fly Boxes

This topic almost seems too obvious to be included here, but there's a special problem: Rust. A waterlogged streamer fly holds *lots* of water and will rust faster than a North-Country pickup truck—weakening the hook and discoloring the fly—unless you take some care. Those lovely looking leather streamer books keep air from getting to soggy flies, and promote rust. The new dense-foam-lined boxes are even worse: When you stick a wet hook into the foam it traps moisture around the hook point and rusts it very quickly. The best solution is a durable plastic box divided into long (not square) compartments in which your streamer flies can rest loosely without having their feathers bent. In all cases, leave your boxes or streamer books open to dry overnight after a day on the river.

Picking a Pattern

3

The low hills of northern Quebec glowed with the fall colors of their alpine shrubs; Labrador tea and lowbush blueberries showing bright orange and green and red on a pale background of caribou moss and lichen and granite. I had waded gingerly through a backwater dotted with car-size boulders to the edge of a huge pool that swirled and eddied black at the bottom of a whitewater chute. It was a perfect setting for really big trout on a streamer fly.

The brook trout were close to spawning, congregating below the rapids through which they'd make their way into more gentle gravel-bottomed tributary streams and their spawning redds. The male fish I'd already seen were in spawning colors, neon displays of brilliant oranges and reds that echoed the fall landscape and belied the fishes' inherent shyness. I was several hundred miles from the nearest road, exploring the northern Cree Indian territories by floatplane. It was likely these trout had never seen an artificial fly of any kind, and I confidently tied on a big Muddler.

A long cast dropped the fly in the dark water along a ledge, and I moved the fly in the current with a gentle rod-tip teasing. There was an orange flash and bulging water when a big brookie turned under the fly, refusing to take. Another smaller fish boiled too, later in the swing, and I picked up to try again. This time I fished the fly slower. It didn't work, although I had several more false rises. A faster retrieve didn't work either, and I was confounded.

These were wilderness brook trout and subject to no fishing pressure. By all accounts in every book I could think of they should have climbed all over any streamer pattern in sight. But they didn't. Over a week's fishing they were just as selective to fly pattern as their suburban cousins far to the south. After a few tries, the answer proved to

21

be a Yellow Marabou Muddler, fished as slowly and with as much feather-twitching as possible. I experimented with streamer patterns over several hundred trout in those few days, and the Yellow Marabou outfished several other conventional patterns by a margin of at least ten to one.

More often than not, I've found all trout to be selective to streamer pattern, although to varying degrees. The extent of this selectivity—or lack of it—can depend on the predominance of a particular forage fish, the proximity to the trout's spawning time, water temperature and color, or even combinations thereof. All of these relate to the important attributes of streamer patterns themselves: color, shape, size, design, and action.

Many writers have used most of these attributes in describing streamer flies, usually ranking them in their relative importance. I should point out that none of a good streamer's characteristics are mutually exclusive. There's also an age-old argument as to whether a fly's imitative qualities are more important than a good presentation to the fish (or vice versa), and once again these aren't mutually exclusive either. Many people become confused by such pointless arguments and concentrate only on a few attributes of fly-pattern selection and fishing instead of combining all of them to best advantage in any given situation. I'll be separating the characteristics of streamer flies in order to explain them, but keep in mind they'll ultimately be used in combination.

Action

Streamer-fly action is the better part of what makes a trout strike in the first place, and this is the action given the fly by the fishermen after the cast is made. Action as it pertains to fly pattern itself is a function of fly materials. Marabou is softer and more flexible than bucktail, for example, and wiggles more in the water of its own accord. Marabou thus has more action. Similar materials with considerable inherent action include rabbit-fur strips and natural long-fibered wool.

The most popular new streamer patterns of the past twenty years or so have been based on these materials. The best-known examples are Dan Byford's Zonker series, based on a rabbit-fur-strip wing, and the

22

Well-known imitative patterns such as the Gray Ghost *(top)* are giving way in most fly boxes to more easily constructed and action-based patterns such as this Black Woolly Bugger. The complete streamer fisherman uses both.

Woolly Bugger, originated by Russell Blessing in 1967 and popularized by Pennsylvania fly tier Barry Beck. The Woolly Bugger is essentially a Woolly Worm with oversize hackle and a long marabou tail. In both cases, the fly materials pulse and undulate seductively in the water, often teasing strikes from otherwise reluctant fish.

Saddle hackles, the traditional winging material of streamer flies, are more flexible and provide more inherent action than bucktail but are less active in the water than marabou plumes or rabbit fur. Many streamer patterns are a combination of bucktail under saddle hackle, which usually makes good use of the hackle's greater action. Saddle-hackle streamers are often more imitative of real baitfish than are other types because of the coloration available in both natural and dyed feathers.

The action of many patterns, including Woolly Buggers, is often enhanced by the addition of Flashabou or Krystal Flash to the wing. These are the proprietary names of very thin, flexible Mylar fibers that are highly reflective and available in a wide range of colors. The difference between the two is that Flashabou fibers are flat while Krystal Flash fibers are full of minute kinks that reflect even more light. Because these fibers are so flexible, they work well when included in small amounts in a larger marabou wing, to give the most common example.

In years past, action was sometimes added to streamers and buck-tails by mechanical means. Herter's, the late and great Minnesota mail-order house, used to sell small wiggling discs that you could tie under the head of your streamer to make it wiggle like a miniature bass plug when pulled through the water. Streamers tied on straight ringed-eye hooks were often used together with a small spinner just ahead of the fly. The spinner's flash attracted fish, and the spinner's vibration gave the fly's wing a fantastic and deadly wiggle. Both of these methods are uncommon today, which is just as well. I think such mechanical artifices are vaguely immoral, and there's nothing vague at all about their not conforming to any "fly-fishing-only" regulations.

A single split shot is added by some people to the leader at the head of the fly to give added action, a technique that works especially well with wiggly marabou flies such as Woolly Buggers. This makes the fly dart up and down in the water when retrieved. As a guest at one of the venerable eastern trout clubs, I joined my host in an afternoon of fooling with reluctant trout that were sipping tiny midges. When we finished, he tied on a big black Woolly Bugger with a split shot at the head and proceeded to drive all the trout in the pool berserk as four or five fish at once almost turned inside out trying to catch the thing. With this method, the fly's success depends more on the jigging effect induced by the added weight than on the angler's manipulative skill. The fly has been turned into a hard-to-cast jig, and it's no longer fly fishing. An ultralight spinning rod would work much better. I have, however, explained the method so you can make your own choices.

Color

Much streamer-fly fishing involves imitating a particular baitfish, and here color serves a major role. Color can also be used to affect the relative visibility of a streamer fly in the water, depending on the color of the water itself.

The baitfishes you want to imitate will change from river to river, within different portions of the same river, and also seasonally to a certain extent. There are a couple of ways to attack this problem. The easiest and most common is simply to use those streamer patterns that have become traditional in the region you happen to be fishing. Thus, a Maine brook-trout man may be using a Gray Ghost to imitate smelt, while the Catskill angler mends a Blacknose Dace through his riffles, and the Rocky Mountain fisherman drifts a sculpin-imitating Spuddler deep in a Green River pool.

That's as far as most people get in determining the color and other attributes of their streamer patterns, and that approach works some of the time. A much better way is to consider the specific baitfishes in a given body of water together with their behavior, size, and coloration. You could start with *McClane's Field Guide to Freshwater Fishes of North America* by A. J. McClane, (1978, Holt, Rinehart and Winston), which offers excellent color illustrations plus information on the distribution and habits of minnows and other baitfishes across the country. Even better, however, is a guidebook to the fishes of a particular state or region that will often indicate which forage fishes are important on a river-by-river and lake-by-lake basis. Two excellent examples are Peter Moyle's *Inland Fishes of California* (1976, University of California Press) and Robert G. Werner's *Freshwater Fishes of New York State* (1980, Syracuse University Press). There are many, many others from which to choose. Call or write your state fish and wildlife department and ask them what guidebook they recommend for your region.

By exploring such books, you'll find a variety of helpful things pertinent to streamer-pattern selection. As just a few examples, the bottom-dwelling darters common east of the Rockies become brilliantly colored during their spawning period of April and May in many trout streams, a time when many trout anglers are first on the water and often fishing streamers. At some times of the year, certain northwestern dace (and also at least one northeastern species) have a brilliant red lateral stripe, which can have some implication for your selection of pattern (and which may account in part for the success of the Spruce-series streamers in western waters, by virtue of their red floss bodies).

Color in nature is often dull and only occasionally brilliant. It's most often found blended in subtle shadings from one hue to another, and this is true of most forage fishes (excepting those in spawning colors just mentioned). Tints of tan, olive, yellow, orange, gray, and black

25

can be found in a simple blacknose dace, for example, while a common shiner blends dark green and olive with blue and silver. The best streamer patterns reflect this sort of coloration through a blending of colors, but in widely available commercial patterns such blending is unfortunately rare. One notable exception is the Little Trout series developed years ago by the late Sam Slaymaker of Pennsylvania, who blended small amounts of bucktail in a range of colors within one wing to approximate the coloration of young brook, brown, or rainbow trout.

Such deliberately imitative streamer and bucktail patterns have unfortunately been few and far between. The Blacknose Dace by the late Art Flick is apt to be the only imitative staple in most fly boxes. Don Gapen's original Muddler Minnow was tied in the 1930s to imitate a sculpin, but even now in all its popularity is rarely fished on the bottom, where sculpins live. Lew Oatman was a superlative fly tier who lived near the New York Battenkill after World War II, and flies like his Battenkill Shiner and Golden Darter can still be found in some pattern books, but rarely in stores. Ernest Schwiebert included eight imitative streamer patterns of his own design in his book *Trout* (1978, E. P. Dutton), which are based on a subtle and very effective blending of colors in a marabou wing. There has been relatively little else in recent years, and in the history of streamer fishing many of the most successful patterns have been accidents.

In addition to imitative considerations, color can affect the visibility of your fly in the water. An all-black fly, of which a black Marabou or black Woolly Bugger are good examples, is the most visible color to trout in turbid water and may be more effective than other patterns for that reason alone. I'll stick my neck out here and say, for example, that black marabou works best in roily water, yellow marabou works best in tea-colored or slightly turbid water, and white marabou is best in clear water. That's been my experience anyway, and I've found it to be just as true in Montana as I have in Maine, with the notable exception of large rainbow trout that often seem to prefer black marabou even in clear spring creeks.

Size and Shape

Size and shape as they pertain to streamer patterns are both important imitative considerations. There's as much difference in silhouette, for example, between a smelt and a sculpin as between an elephant and an eel. Trout readily discern the difference, and you must consider this in tying or buying your streamer patterns.

One good example is the classic Gray Ghost streamer originated in 1924 by the late Carrie Stevens at Upper Dam, Maine. I've studied many of her own dressings over the years, including numerous Gray Ghosts, and they are universally elegant flies—long, slim, and showing a blending of colors both subtle and skillful. Most of her streamers were smelt imitations and accurately reflect the subtle colors and slim profile of these baitfish. For example, her slim saddle-hackle wings were typically tied along the side of the floss body, rather than on top, to keep a slim profile and also so that the body color would show through the wing as a *blended* color muted by the color of the wing itself.

The Gray Ghost streamer, because it is so minnowlike in a generic way, is in general use all over the world as a streamer pattern. Most commercial versions of this old standby are horribly inferior to the originals simply because these flies are commonly tied now with stubby saddle hackles on top of the hook instead of slim ones along the side. The slim profile has been lost in the translation, and so has much of the pattern's potential effectiveness.

Getting used to the idea that most streamer patterns are supposed to *look* like a little fish can help with your basic selections. As another example, sculpins (and darters) are common bottom-dwelling fishes that are a favorite food of brown trout, in particular. Sculpins are rather like little gargoyles with big flat heads, goggly eyes, prominent pectoral fins, and very slim bodies that taper abruptly to the tail. The shape is very distinctive, and this is reflected in the evolution of imitative streamer patterns. The famous Muddler Minnow was first tied to imitate sculpins but is usually more minnow-shaped than a sculpin. The Spuddler, originated by Dan Bailey and Red Monical in Montana, was a next step, but the most imitative and commercially available patterns are now the Wool-Head Sculpin and the Whitlock Sculpin, which accurately reflect this fish's unique shape and coloration. Both can be deadly when fished near the *bottom* of pools, where both sculpins and big brown trout live.

Size is almost as important as shape, and here many fishermen are missing a bet. Most people seem to get a few streamer patterns in

27

hook sizes 6 and 4 and let it go at that. In many shops, particularly eastern and midwestern shops, it's often hard to find streamers bigger than size 4. In small streams and brooks I'm often using streamers down to a size 12, and in big water I may sometimes use flies as large as 3/0 that are almost six inches long. You should consider size in matching a prevalent baitfish, in matching young-of-the-year baitfish, and in sometimes using an outsize fly while hoping to attract larger trout.

It's easy to look in the quieter waters of the river you happen to be fishing, note that the dace are two to three inches long, and then use a streamer of appropriate size. But sometimes the size question is more subtle. As one example, threadfin shad, which have been introduced in numerous lakes and reservoirs as forage fish, tend to school according to their size. If schools of two-inch-long shad are prevalent, the trout may actually become selective in feeding on shad of this size, and it can take considerable experimentation on your part to make your flies fit this natural pattern.

Young-of-the-year baitfish are commonly overlooked by streamer fishermen, although imitating them is obviously a good bet. Large schools of juvenile yellow perch, for example, are often prime forage for various trout species in late spring where larger streams enter lakes and ponds. In rivers, trout are often feeding on young (and thus small) dace and other forage fishes and even on trout and salmon fry or parr. One well-known example is the "hatch" of millions of salmon fry on Alaskan rivers in June, upon which some gargantuan rainbows feed avidly. In these cases and many others, deliberately using small streamers can really pay off.

Design

Although a fly's pattern is a simple recipe-list of materials, a fly's design is the purposeful manner of its construction, which in turn can be applied to a variety of patterns. The stereotypical streamer design—a long wing tied at the head of a long-shanked hook—means that the end of the wing can become tangled under the hook in casting. If this happens on one out of three casts, it means that one-third of your fishing time is being wasted. Happily, there are a number of design

The wing of conventionally tied streamer patterns can become tangled in the hook, spoiling your cast. Matuka-style *(lower fly)* tying binds the wing to the hook shank and eliminates tangling.

solutions to this problem, some of which are independent of fly pattern and widely adaptable.

One answer to the tangling problem is to tie or buy streamers with wings that don't extend past the hook bend. In this case, even if the wing does bend under the hook shank momentarily, it won't become caught and will thus fish normally. The late Bill Edson's famous Light and Dark Tiger bucktails were originally tied in this fashion, and there's no reason why any conventional streamer pattern can't be tied this way, although most aren't.

Another solution is to bind down the wing at both ends of the hook shank so the wing can't move under the hook. Zonker-style ties use this method. A similar design is used in Matuka-style streamers in which the feather wing is bound to the body over its whole length by ribbing. Matukas are an old New Zealand design that enjoyed a renaissance on American waters in the 1970s and are still popular and effective. A third design solution is found in Woolly Buggers and

29

some leech patterns in which the "wing" is actually an elongated tail tied in at the hook bend to be generally tangle-free.

There are some other design considerations you might encounter. Conventional saddle-hackle wings are made with the feathers' concave sides facing one another to produce a slim profile. Making the fly with the hackles' convex sides facing one another causes the feathers to flare outward and to pulse and breathe when twitched, giving added action to the fly. Another and seldom-used design puts all the hackle-feather wing on one *side* of the fly. When retrieved, this unbalanced design spins and darts erratically in the water. The action is terrific, but the twisting will raise hell with your leader.

Across and Downstream

4

The Basic Technique

B asic technique in streamer fishing is so simple that a novice can take trout by this method *before* learning how to fly cast. If you're a beginner, it's a good way to catch the fish that provide the encouragement for you to keep learning. If you're teaching someone else, it's a good way to start them off.

Find a spot on your trout stream where a long riffle or whitewater chute empties into a large pool. Trout will almost always be concentrated at this spot. I'll assume for now that you're using the nine-foot rod I suggested earlier, a floating line, a nine-foot leader tapered to 2X, and an unweighted #6 Black Ghost streamer, which will be easy to see in the water because of its white wing.

Position yourself in or at the edge of the shallow fast water a few feet above the point at which it shelves into the pool's deeper water. Pull fifteen or twenty feet of line off the reel, point the rod downstream, and shake the rod tip back and forth to pull the line through the guides. The current will carry the line, leader, and fly down into the pool, and then will straighten the line so the fly is hanging in the current.

Now put the line under the index finger of your rod hand and use that finger to hold the line firmly by squeezing it against the rod grip. With your other hand (left hand for right-handed people) grasp the line behind your rod hand. Point the rod tip at the fly. Relax your rod-hand grip slightly and use the other hand to pull in six inches of line in one rapid motion. Stop pulling and tighten your rod-hand grip simultaneously. Your fly, as you could probably see, darted forward in the current and then stopped, just like a real minnow. Repeat the process, pausing for only a brief second between strips, until you've retrieved almost all of the line and the fly has progressed upstream out of the

The spot where a riffle or chute dumps into a deeper pool is an ideal place to station a beginner, allowing him to fish straight downstream over a concentration of trout.

deeper water where the trout live. Shake out all the line once again so the current carries it down into the pool, and start over again in the same fashion.

Sooner or later—probably sooner—a trout will come up and slash at the fly. The fish will likely hook itself if it hits the fly solidly because the line is perfectly straight and you're holding it firmly with your rod hand. If the fish is relatively small, you should be able to play and land it in the fast water without moving. A larger fish should be allowed to pull line from the reel while you move around into quieter water where you can play, land, and release the fish more easily.

That's all there is to it, and suddenly you're catching trout even though you still face the hurdle of learning how to cast. The same method will also sometimes work with wet flies or nymphs, but I like to start people with a light-colored streamer that's easier for a novice to see in the water. This method can work on clear spring creeks as well as on more typical freestone streams, and can even be effective on hard-fished water such as the no-kill areas of New York's Beaverkill. The most important ingredients, once again, are fast water dumping into a pool plus a good concentration of trout.

That's not, however, all there is to streamer fishing. It's a method that can be enormously subtle and demanding of skill, and in the rest of this book we'll explore some of the streamer tactics that make it so.

Streamer flies are most commonly fished by casting across and downstream at some angle to the current. The current's pressure on the line forces the fly to swim across the flow and to stop when the line straightens below the fisherman. Unless you're trying to work over a particular spot, a couple of downstream steps are taken between casts so the water is covered by a series of concentric fly swings as you progress downstream. The fly's action in the water, the speed at which it travels across the current, and the fly's swimming depth can all be controlled by the fisherman to suit various circumstances.

Down-and-across fishing is among the least demanding of our assorted streamer tactics. It's the easiest way to cover a lot of water—and fish, presumably—and offers the distinct advantage of working with the current. It's a pleasant rhythm of casting on the first warm days of spring, wading downstream in the current, and pumping cast after cast to the opposite bank. If the water has warmed sufficiently so the trout are aggressive and will chase the moving fly, it's a productive method, too.

There are a couple of drawbacks, though, to be considered before we get too far into the method itself. Most baitfish don't spend their time swimming across the currents of an entire river. Rather, they dart, swim, feed, and rest around a particular eddy, shelf, or pocket in the current. Thus the basic down-and-across method isn't especially imitative of baitfish behavior. It's a lazy method, also, or so it becomes for many people who often fish streamers this way only because it's the easiest way. There are some other productive—and more demanding—methods that often work better, which we'll explore in the next chapter. For now, and with an understanding of some of the problems involved, we can find out how to make the most of streamer

33

fishing downstream.

You can spend your day casting across stream, let the current pull the fly around through a series of casts, and take fish occasionally. But the sooner you start controlling your casts, the more fish you'll catch. The first step in this process is to consider fly speed. Veteran Atlantic-salmon fishermen know that controlling their fly's swimming speed is paramount in attracting salmon, and it's just as important in trout fishing with streamers. In general—and for trout (not necessarily salmon)—slower is better.

If you cast directly across a current, the line will develop a large downstream curve or "belly" that will swing the fly around quickly. If you cast at about a forty-five-degree angle downstream, the belly will be smaller and the fly will usually swing more slowly. At the other extreme, when you cast straight downstream there's no line belly at all, and of course the fly doesn't swing in the current either. After a few experimental casts, it should be evident that the straighter across the current you cast, the faster the fly will swing. Conversely, the greater the downstream angle of your presentation, the slower your fly will swim.

You can put this knowledge to immediate use in fishing. In the turbulent white water at the head of a pool, where many trout often feed, an across-stream cast will cause the current to rip the fly through the water at an absurdly high speed. Cast quartering downstream here, so that your fly swings through the fast water more slowly and at a speed appearing more natural and thus more appealing to the fish. When you get down to the slower water near the end of the pool, a downstream cast may move the fly too slowly in the current. Now you can cast at a greater angle across the current to speed the fly up.

Having made your cross-current cast at an appropriate angle, do the following immediately: Put the line under the index finger of your rod hand and hold it firmly. Grab the line (behind your rod hand) with your other hand. Point the rod tip directly at the fly, and *keep it pointed at the fly* while fishing out the cast. Having done these three things, you're ready for a strike at any point. If you forget these things and stand there gawking at the wonderful cast you just made, you won't be able to hook a fish when it hits your fly.

While fishing the big Battenkill below Shushan, New York, last spring, I lost an immense brown trout by not following my own ad-

I'm standing in the middle of a long riffle, allowing the current to swing my streamer over the edge—marked by arrows on the photograph—where the shallow riffle drops into deep water. This is always a good location for big trout.

vice. I found a spot where the current slid quickly over a shallow gravel shelf into a deep corner hole and positioned myself so an across-stream cast would swing a streamer over the shelf and into deep water. I made the cast and then got lazy, just holding the line in my left hand instead of holding it firmly in my right as I've described. Just as the streamer swung into the deeper water there was a big golden flash and a terrific yank on the line, which pulled it from my grip. The trout made a high-speed run straight downstream on a to-tally slack line. By the time I recovered, the hook had come free. Had I been holding the line correctly, I'm sure I would have caught the fish.

Pointing the rod tip directly at the fly during the cast and following the fly with the rod tip during the swing accomplishes a couple of things. First, this reduces the size of the line belly in the current and thus slows the fly somewhat. Second, it allows you to respond more quickly to a strike—something that's hard to do when your rod tip is high in the air or way off to one side. It's a good habit to get into, although there are some exceptions that I describe in the next chapter.

Having set up your cast to produce a desirable fly speed, you can start manipulating the fly to make it more lifelike. There are a couple of ways to do this, usually used in combination. You can retrieve the line in short, abrupt strips with your free hand stripping in line from behind your rod hand. Or you can simply raise and lower or twitch the rod tip slightly and intermittently. In either case, the fly will speed up and slow down in the course of its swing, much like a minnow starts and stops as it swims. Now your fly seems much more alive than if it's just being pulled across the current at a constant speed. These pulsing motions also allow the fly's materials much greater movement in the current, making the fly itself more lifelike.

Timing your twitches or strips can be a little tricky, and putting the whole thing to music in your mind can be helpful. The basic retrieve is in waltz time: *twitch*-two-three, *twitch*-two-three, with the streamer just swinging or even dead-drifting on the last two counts. It usually helps to vary your retrieve from cast to cast—even on the same cast—until you find one that works best. On some days the trout will come better to a faster cha-cha (one-two-*twitch-twitch-twitch*) or some other variation. The point always is to start and stop the fly in a teasing fashion. The movement seems to attract the trout, and you'll find most of your strikes happen just *after* a twitch when the trout has a nearly stationary target.

Down-and-across streamer fishing has a moment of truth, and that's when the cast straightens out in the current below you. Many strikes occur at this instant, and for several reasons. Often the moving fly will have stopped abruptly near a trout, and this sudden change in motion can trigger a hit. It's also common for a trout to follow a swinging streamer a long way across stream, nose to the feathers but undecided. Once again the abrupt stop may force the fish to make up its mind. In any case, be ready as the cast straightens out below you, and don't pull the fly from the water immediately for another cast. Make a few strips straight upstream first, just in case.

Other things being equal, the fisherman whose fly spends the most time in productive water will catch the most fish. Most people fish trout rivers from the shallow side because it's usually more accessible. When fishing down and across with a streamer, this often means that the fly is swinging into unproductive water. If I can, I fish a pool or bend from the deep side, quartering my casts downstream and letting the fly swing into deeper water along the bank where the fish are. After the fly swing is completed, I can teasingly retrieve the streamer back up along the edge of the deep bank. Each cast I make in this fashion spends twice as long in a productive area than it would were I over in the shallows on the other side.

So far this discussion has pertained mostly to floating-line streamer fishing, but there are times when you have to go deep to take fish. The obvious case is reaching fish in deeper water. Another is in fishing imitations of bottom-dwelling fish such as sculpins and darters. Yet another—and the most common—is when the water is relatively cold and the fish lethargic, reluctant to chase a fly on the surface. This is typical of the early season on most trout streams.

The sort of sinking line or sinking shooting head you use will usually depend on the depth and speed of the water. I usually cast either one down and across stream, and then let the line drift, swing, and sink to near the bottom of a pool or run below me. When the line straightens out, I want the fly to be as deep as possible so I can twitch it back upstream slowly near the bottom.

If I've cast slightly downstream, I mend the rear or running portion of the line back upstream or across stream to let the front end sink

Swinging a Black Marabou streamer through the head of this pool on a sinking-tip line produced a rainbow trout that weighed in at eight pounds before it was released.

quickly. I may feed slack line into the drift for the same reason. I hold the rod very high and lower it slowly as the forward portion of the line swings and sinks, using the raised rod to try to keep the current from pulling on the rearward line and thus pulling the sinking portion back toward the surface. By the time the swinging sunken portion is starting to straighten out, my rod tip is pointed down at where I think the fly is and I'm ready for a strike. If no fish hits, I strip the fly slowly back upstream until the shooting head or sinking tip comes back to the surface, at which point I can pick up for another cast. When the line is straight downstream, the current tends to buoy the sinking portion upward, which is why I usually use extra-fast-sinking sinking tips or shooting heads to keep maximum depth. If I sometimes hook bottom in a deep pool or run, I know I'm right on target.

I've moved out of the riffle and down into the pool. Here I'm fishing more directly across stream to swing my streamer in the deeper current where fish are holding along the rocks.

Sunken-line streamer fishing requires enormous concentration. You can't see your drift as you can with a floating line, so you have to visualize. I create a moving picture of my deeply sunken fly in my mind and use that intuitive guide in controlling the drift. I've learned by experience exactly what the line vibrations feel like as the streamer ticks along the bottom rocks. When the ticks stop, the water has deepened, so I feed a little slack to drop the fly deeper. When it comes, the strike is sometimes hard, at other times it is a gentle pull that takes all my attention to even feel. I sometimes have a sore back after an hour or two of fishing this way; the soreness comes from bending over slightly with muscles tensed, concentrating on swimming a streamer I can't see.

Of the many tricks to down-and-across, there's one other I'll pass along here. It uses your long nine-foot rod to maximum advantage with either a floating or sinking line. If you reach as far as you can to one side with your rod, your rod and arm extension may be about eleven feet. By extending the same way on the opposite side, you have a range of more than twenty feet across the stream within which you can place the rod tip to control where the fly swings and stops. Thus, instead of swinging the fly quickly past a boulder in the downstream current, you can reach to one side and have the fly stop anywhere relative to the boulder (or other target) you wish. Having stopped the fly, you can tease it back upstream for a foot or two and then let it drop slowly back. Then, move your rod to the side a little and then back, giving the fly a teasing motion all the while. This is more like a real minnow's behavior than anything we've yet done in this chapter, and it can drive the trout nuts.

Stutters and Stops
Advanced Technique

F all River in northern California is one of the world's biggest spring creeks. Its source percolates upward through the pre-historic lava beds north of Mount Lassen at Thousand Springs, and the smooth flow meanders for mile after gentle mile through a fertile, flat basin before joining the Pit River near Fall River Mills and flowing on into the Sacramento system. Wild rice is a cash crop in this region, grown in large paddies on the valley floors, and I sometimes see a solitary man with a rifle out walking the dikes, looking for musk-rats and their destructive tunneling.

The river is smooth, fertile, and wonderfully clear. Access is limited by private farmland and posted club holdings, and most who fish here use small prams with electric outboard motors to work up or down the gentle currents at will. There are long stretches of shallower water over gently waving underwater weeds where large pods of selective rainbows sip mayfly spinners in the delicate fashion common to spring-creek trout. It seems unlikely water for a streamer fly.

"Monsters. There are monster trout in these holes," Tim Bedford said as we drifted through a deep bend. The water was dark blue-black down as far as I could see, and I couldn't see bottom. Bedford had just retired from a long engineering career with Kaiser in Oakland, and his travels for that company allowed more than forty years of fishing all over the world. In retirement he turned to bamboo-rod building and made a small number of extraordinary fine-casting rods before an untimely death. He kept a club membership on Fall River for many years, where I fished as his guest.

"Once in a while a club or clubs will have a fishing contest here," he explained, "and the biggest fish almost always came to big Black Marabous fished deep in these holes." The technique as I learned it from

41

Michigan angler Dick Pobst working a streamer down and across against the fish-holding snags and pockets along the far *(right, as you view the photograph)* bank.

Vern Gallup using a fast-sinking line to work his fly slowly and almost straight downstream through a deep and fast outlet of a big pool. Big migrating trout often hold in such water.

him was relatively simple and has accounted for a number of large trout over the years on other waters, too. Like streamer fishing with a floating line, it involves a swinging fly, but instead of swinging the fly across the currents, the fly swing is vertical, fishing the river's currents from the bottom to the surface.

I tied on a black Woolly Bugger and cast the fast-sinking-tip line about sixty feet straight upstream from a deep corner. As the line drifted back toward me I kept retrieving slack and mending the floating portion upstream, being careful not to put any tension on the sinking portion so as to get maximum depth. Finally the sinking portion was drifting—deep and out of sight—past my own position, and I simply stopped feeding line. The current then put tension on the sunken portion, starting to move it upward as I teased the rod tip and gave life to the feathers. There was a hard yank almost straight down, and I almost fell over. The fish pulled line hard and then came up cartwheeling near the other bank. The rainbow measured twenty-three inches in the net, and shot back down into the darkness when we slipped it free.

When I describe advanced streamer tactics, I mean those methods other than conventional down-and-across fishing. Such tactics are a matter of deciding how you want your fly to behave—and where—and then determining a way, or ways, of making it happen.

One key to fishing for stream trout with streamers and bucktails lies in getting the fly in the vicinity of a fish and keeping it there with the appearance of a natural. If you read nothing else this season and go forth with that one sentence on your mind and some streamers on your vest, you will be likely to do well. Once again, get the fly in the vicinity of a fish and keep it there. Consider the following example.

You're rigged up with a blue dun Matuka streamer of about the same size and coloration as the dominant forage fish in this stream. Across the stream against the bank is a large rock, behind which is an eddy about four feet in diameter through which a portion of the current turns before shooting downstream. That old feeling in your stomach tells you with no uncertainty that there's a good trout in that dark hole.

Keeping your fly near the fish means you have to prevent the current from pulling your line—and the fly—out of the neighborhood. You have to control your line. The less line you have out, the better you can control it, so get as close as you comfortably can to that eddy without scaring whatever may be in there. Twenty-five to thirty feet away should be fine, with the eddy directly across stream from your position.

Soak your fly in the water so that it will sink when you make your cast. Make your false casts gently to avoid drying out the fly. If you have to tug and yank the line to get the fly to sink when you should be fishing it, you're wasting time.

You *know* there's a trout there. The object is to keep the fly swimming naturally in front of him for as long as you can. Aim your cast so the fly will drop in the downstream portion of the eddy. While the line is straightening out in the air, make an upstream mend. When the fly and line hit the water, the line will already be mended. (After power has been applied on the forward cast and while the line is straightening out in the air, move the rod tip sharply with a semicircular motion in the direction you wish the line to be mended when it lands on the water.)

If I had to pick a day for streamer fishing, it would be gray, foggy, and drizzling rain, when the lack of sunlight can make bigger fish more aggressive, as this brown trout demonstrated with a little help from me.

Here's a common situation in many pools. The current along the rocks
holds the fish, and that same current is of a different speed than that
where I'm standing. I'll start by casting almost straight across stream, and
work to keep the fly along the rocks.

The fly, having landed at the lower end of the eddy, is being carried upstream. The line on the water in front of you is being carried rapidly downstream. If you don't do something—and fast—the current on the line belly is going to pull the fly out of the productive water and send it swinging rapidly downstream.

Get the rod tip up—high. Get the line belly out of the main current flow and keep it in the eddy. Twitch the rod tip gently. A little twitch makes the hackles pulsate: Your imitation comes alive. You stop; it stops. It rests and drifts a few inches. Twitch again, gently. The fly swims a few inches and then rests.

By now you've probably got the rod tip as high as you comfortably can and the accumulated slack between the rod and the fly is starting to be affected by the main current. This is where most people give up. But don't. You are, coincidentally, in the perfect position for a roll cast back into the eddy. Use an *underpowered* roll cast that won't actually lift the fly from the water but will throw some leader and line back into the eddy and get you out of that awkward, reaching-for-the-sky position. Now you've done it, so get the rod tip up again and the line belly out of the current. Twitch gently, then rest for a split second. Twitch. Rest.

The fly has been swimming in lifelike fashion around the eddy for a couple of minutes. Your arm is starting to hurt from the strain of keeping that rod tip up and making those underpowered roll casts at the right split second.

The fly pulsates gently and rests. Pulsates. Rests. A brown trout resting on the bottom can't stand it any longer. You've got a slashing strike; the sore arm is worth it.

Let's go back and examine a few things now that the fish has been landed and released. Obviously, you won't always be directly across stream from the suspected lie of a trout. But I illustrated two related tools—mending and an underpowered roll cast—that you can use in many other situations, always with the goal of keeping that fly in productive water for as long as possible. I'm sure that most anglers can take that basic bit of advice and start to adapt it to situations as they occur, be they straight across stream or not.

Here are some further refinements. Suppose you'd swum that fly around the eddy until your arm couldn't take it anymore and you hadn't had a hit. One possible answer depends on what appears to be

In this case, by holding my rod high as the fly drifts along the rocks I prevent the current near me from catching the line and influencing the drift. As soon as I can't reach any higher, I'll mend the line upstream, always with the goal of holding the fly in position near the fish.

This brown trout was about sixteen inches long, and hit my streamer only after I'd been swimming the fly over him constantly for about two minutes in the course of a single cast.

almost a universal relationship between predator and prey. Most predators will choose a victim within a group if that victim is behaving abnormally. For a trout and some baitfish, that can mean a couple of things. The trout may single out one baitfish if that baitfish tries desperately to escape. The trout may also attack if aroused by the behavior of a slowly moving baitfish that is markedly different from normal. Anglers fishing with streamers can take advantage of both of those situations.

Let's take the first example of desperate escape and apply it to the eddy fished earlier. Instead of the fly swimming about normally near the surface, let it sink slowly as long as possible. Then, before drag starts, pull the fly to the surface in a series of very rapid twitches. If the fly makes a wake or skips along the top toward the end of the retrieve, so much the better—so do baitfish when pursued.

If your trout hadn't responded earlier, he may well do so now, and viciously! You should realize that you'll have considerable difficulty in retrieving the fly fast enough to take it away from a trout that wants it badly, so don't be bashful with the speed of your retrieve. A portion of the success of this method lies in making those rapid twitches at a

49

consistent speed. The rapidity will trigger the fish's response, while the consistency will let him home-in on the fly.

If you *still* haven't had a hit, there's another trick that works often enough to make it worthwhile. If you're using a standard streamer or bucktail, loop the leader under the wing. If you're using a Matuka-style streamer, tie it on with a riffling hitch. The object in either case is to make the fly spin or vibrate unnaturally as it *slowly* passes through the eddy. That, sometimes, is more than a poor trout can stand. Be careful though, because after a few tries this may start to twist your leader.

In the sort of situation I've just described, it's fairly common for a trout to start for the fly and refuse it at the last second, showing in the water as a boil or flash near the fly. This happens most often when fishing with bright wiggly flies such as marabou streamers. There are two schools of thought on what you should do next. One holds that the best next step is to put the fly right back over the fish, but to retrieve it either faster or more slowly, hoping that a speed change will make the fish come again. Sometimes this works, but more often it doesn't.

I think it's better to change flies immediately. I might simply use the same pattern in a smaller (rarely larger) size, but I more often switch to a more imitative pattern—from a white Marabou to a badger Matuka is a good example. Sometimes, too, the answer requires fishing more deeply, more slowly, or both. I don't always catch the fish by making these sorts of changes, but I often do. When I don't, I always believe it's my fault for not having thought of some critical factor. The trout, after all, has already shown its interest.

Many streamer-fly casts show the fly to the trout as a quartering or end-on view. A fly is head-into the current as it swings across, and most trout won't be able to see the entire fly. There has been a recurring suggestion made by various writers that the fly be presented broadside to the fish, which I think is a sound tactic. I say "recurring" because the method was described by John Alden Knight in 1940, and the same technique was popularized by the late Joe Brooks more than thirty years later as what he called the "broadside float." The method is superficially similar to the so-called "greased line" method of Atlantic-salmon wet-fly fishing, in which a series of line mends are used to control both the fly's swimming speed and its orientation in the cur-

Casting straight to the bank and making a series of very fast line mends upstream may hold the fly long enough in that brushy pocket to produce a fish, in spite of the torrential current.

rent. In any case, it's now the streamer technique I use more often than any other.

I'll assume for the moment that I'm standing in the middle of a fairly large river fishing to the far bank with a floating line. Most of the trout will be holding positions along that bank. I cast straight across stream, or perhaps slightly up, and drop the streamer an inch or two from the bank. I have a few seconds to twitch the fly a couple of times before the current threatens to swing the growing line belly downstream. I make an upstream mend and again have a few seconds to twitch the fly a time or two straight toward me and perpendicular to the current flow. By a series of mends and intermittent twitches, I'm fishing the fly broadside to the current—and the fish—almost straight across the river.

By this method, the fly itself stutters forward and stops, drifting downstream slightly with the stops and stuttering forward with the twitches and line mends. As Jack Knight pointed out fifty years ago, the strikes—when they come—are apt to be more subtle than the typical slashing rise to a rapidly swinging fly. Even large trout may take with a leisurely and confident roll on a broadside drift. With all the twitching and line-mending, this is very apt to happen on a slack line, and you'll have to watch your fly carefully to respond in time and not miss the fish.

The technique can be used instead of simple down-and-across fishing to cover a long stretch of water with repetitive casts. It is most easily done in the broad easy currents of rivers like Vermont's Battenkill or Michigan's Au Sable, or along the edges of pools in bigger rivers like Montana's Yellowstone where Brooks made the technique famous. The same method will work well in faster, rougher water, but you'll be working that much harder with your upstream-line-mending to keep the fly working correctly.

Although a river can be covered to the limit of your casting range by this method, I find it helpful and more productive to use every cast and drift to a specific target. Most commonly the target is the stretch of quieter water a few feet wide against the far bank. Trout typically favor such a spot as holding water, and I'll mend the line on every cast to keep the fly working in this area as much as possible. There may also be downed trees, undercut stumps, rocks, ledges, or eddies as targets on the far bank, and each of these will require a slightly unique

Slower and shallow water this time, so I wade carefully and use a long cast across stream to work over the trout along the far, brushy bank.

Bill Herrick working to put his streamer right against the deep bank and mending to keep it from being pulled away by the current. Mending line here will float the streamer broadside to the bankside fish, a method popularized by the late Joe Brooks.

blend of line-mending and fly-twitches to be most effectively covered. The same holds true for similar midstream targets. The method is generically simple, but the subtle variations you impart to each and every cast are what catches the fish.

Advanced streamer tactics are the tactics of adaptation. The only limits are your imagination and your ability to cast and manipulate your line. The effectiveness of any given method on a particular day and stretch of river will be self-evident: The trout will respond or they won't. If the fish aren't coming to one method, the novice quits, and therein lies the difference.

Float-Fishing
with Streamers

6

B eing able to fish a larger trout river from a boat is a mixed blessing. The boat fisherman covers much more water than does a
wading angler and reaches many spots a wading angler can't. But the
boat fisherman is usually moving past any given target fairly quickly,
often too fast to cover well those spots a wading fisherman might
cover more carefully and productively. I have often, for example,
caught as many or more trout as large or larger in a day's wading on
Montana's Madison River than I have in a day's float trip on the same
river.

Floating is also sometimes the *only* way to really fish a river, either
because some productive stretches are too much of a distant walk—as
with some areas of the Madison—or because shoreline access is limited by posted land, as with many rivers in the West and elsewhere. In
any case, fishing in moving water from a boat and with streamers calls
for some special tricks, a few of which we'll examine here.

Conventional streamer strategy is based on the wading angler stationary in a stream. This means one end of the line is stationary also,
and the angler has to mend and manipulate his line in the flow to
control the fly. In float fishing, *both* ends of the line are moving. The
angler's boat is moving downstream and so is the fly, often in currents
of different speeds. Line-control problems thus become different and
sometimes complex.

The kind of boat you're fishing from will also make a difference.
Most drift boats—also called MacKenzie River boats—as are commonly used in the Rockies and West are sufficiently stable to allow
casting and fishing while standing up, which is by far the easiest way.
You'll have to fish sitting down from an inflatable raft, common on
many western rivers, or from a canoe, as commonly done in the

Fishing from a MacKenzie-style drift boat on a western river usually means casting repetitively to bankside targets.

Northeast. For most of this chapter, I'll assume you're standing in the bow of a drift boat being rowed by a good guide on a larger river.

Many drift boats have knee-locks at the bow, which enable you to brace yourself while standing. There's usually a small deck right in front of you to hold your loose fly line. When you start, strip off line and make a cast of fifty feet or so. Then strip in line so it falls in large loose coils on the deck, and you're ready to start fishing. The guide will be right behind you in the center of the boat, rowing upstream to slow and control the boat's downstream drift and to stay a comfortable cast away from the bank toward which you'll be fishing.

Assume for the moment you're a right-handed caster fishing the left bank as you face downstream. Use a high backcast so the plane of your forward cast can be aimed downward toward the water along the bank. Use the full bend of the rod in casting so your rod ends up low to the water after your forward power stroke and the line is perfectly straight between your rod and the fly. You should be casting accurately enough so your fly lands within an inch or two of the bank (or any other target) every time.

The trout will almost always be lying within a foot or so of the bank or other cover, and—other things being equal—he who can cast most accurately will catch the most fish. On some rivers, especially popular rivers like the Madison or Big Horn in Montana, the trout are treated to a daylong parade of drift boats constantly working the same banks. When streamer fishing (and with other fly types, too) if you cast your fly right on target to the back of an eddy, behind a stump, or through a hole in the brush, you'll probably be covering water—and catching trout—the other boats haven't. This sort of accurate casting comes with long practice and tackle properly balanced to the size and weight of the fly you're fishing. Being aware of its importance, however, can be of help to anyone.

Now you've gotten the fly next to the bank, and your line is straight

Brown trout of this size are most commonly caught on streamers as opposed to other fly types. This fish came from Montana's Big Horn on a Dark Spruce streamer in October.

so you're in control of the fly and ready for a strike. The fly is drifting broadside in the current, paralleling the downstream motion of the boat. By working the rod tip a little and stripping line with your line hand as need be, you can give the fly some life. Try to keep it in productive water for as long as possible, which means near the bank and not midriver. If the current is smooth and of constant flow between you and the bank, you should be able to keep the fly alive and drifting there for several feet. More typically, the current speed is varied, and you'll have to mend line up or downstream to keep the fly in position for as long as possible.

Sooner or later, of course, you'll have to pick up for another cast, and this introduces another problem. There are usually fishy-looking spots every few feet along the bank, and trying to cover every one of them as you're drifting along is exhausting. The first few times I tried this, I wound up casting like a machine gun for a couple of hours and was ruined for the rest of the day. As the boat drifts, keep looking ahead at possible targets. You'll have to keep picking one—and passing up others—in order to fish that one properly.

This problem and its solution offers a bonus for an alert fisherman in the back of the boat. Two fly fishermen often fish simultaneously from a drift boat, and the caster in the bow always has first whack at a choice spot. Since it's impossible for the bow caster to fish *every* good-looking spot, all the rearward fisherman has to do is to watch where the bow person casts and fish where he or she doesn't. Sometimes the bow fisherman will raise a fish that doesn't touch the fly, and because of the boat's drift can't cast back to the fish. Again, the alert fisherman in the stern has an excellent shot at catching the very same fish.

There's one method of manipulating a streamer fly that works especially well when drift fishing, although it can be used by wading anglers to lesser effect. Mel Krieger, the San Francisco fly-casting instructor, described this to me after having taken a float trip with Tom Morgan, who owns the Winston Rod Company in Twin Bridges, Montana. I haven't fished with Tom nor seen him use this technique, but I fooled around with it a little based on Mel's description and thus found a way of giving super action to a streamer fly without pulling it too far from the bank.

One aspect of fly-rod physics means that when you push the rod sharply downward, the tip flips up before following the rod down, and

Even though fishing from the rear of the boat and thus getting the second shot at the best spots, I was able to hold my own by watching and then fishing where the bow caster didn't.

vice versa. When the fly is drifting close to the bank on a fairly tight line, if you flip your rod downward sharply, the up-flipping tip causes the fly to dart forward a short distance. As the tip recoils, it gives a little slack, which causes the fly to stop just as abruptly. All this can take place without your having to retrieve any line—or at most just enough to keep line control—and the starts and stops of the fly are much more abrupt than you can achieve by simply stripping line. It's a deadly and simple secret.

Many of the tactics I described for wading anglers in the previous chapters apply also to float fishing, and here's one example of such an adaptation. Suppose you see a large rock downstream and a few feet out from the bank. Commonly, trout will be holding behind and on either side of the rock, waiting to nab whatever food the current offers. The typical float fisherman will drop a cast in the eddy behind the rock and may often take a fish in so doing.

But more than a dozen boats have already fished this rock today, so let's try something different. Cast your fly upstream of the rock and near the bank. As you float abreast of the rock, use an underpowered roll cast to throw some slack over the rock and to place your line downstream of the rock at the same time. Now you can raise your rod and swim the streamer downstream around the far side of the rock and through the eddy from the bank side. Chances are the fish will never have seen a streamer presented in this way (unless I'm in the boat you can see downstream) and you may get a violent strike that you wouldn't have gotten with a more conventional cast.

When a right-handed caster fishes the right bank (or a left-hander the left side), both the caster and the guide can be in danger of being struck and hooked by the cast. In this case, a conventional backcast brings the fly over the boat between the caster and guide. Guides are a little touchy about this and rightly so; it's no fun having to yank a big hook out of your ear or neck. Using your right arm across your body in a backhanded casting motion is too strenuous for a full day's fishing, and I use a different solution that Phil Wright showed me years ago during a Big Hole River float trip.

Hold your rod vertically with your arm raised so your hand is about level with your right ear. Keep your hand there, but tip your rod off-vertical to the left. The rod should be at about a forty-five-degree angle, which means the tip clears your left side by several feet. Make your casting strokes from this position, which puts your casting plane back over the bow of the boat where it belongs. This also means you can put some body English into your backhand casting, bending forward on the forward cast, for example, for both muscle and emphasis.

With both this method and conventional casting, there's another little trick you can add that can make a difference. If you stop your forward cast abruptly, or even pull back on the rod slightly as the cast straightens out, the line will turn over with more than normal force. This makes the waterlogged and heavy streamer hit the water with a good, hard *splat*. On some days this seems to get the fish's attention and can bring a near-immediate strike. On other days, it just scares the trout. You'll have to experiment.

This float-fishing discussion has been limited to fishing with a floating line. I almost never use a sinking line while drift-fishing. I enjoy having the trout come to a big streamer that I can see, and generally feel I need the line control given by a floating line to drift-fish effectively. When you come to a big, deep hole that just demands to be bottom-fished with a sinking line, ask the guide if he'll beach the boat down below so you can walk back up and fish it properly.

Girdlebugs and Yuk Bugs are common offerings by most float fishermen in the West these days. I rather like fishing these rubber-legged ersatz nymphs and took a number of small brown trout that way on the lower Madison not long ago with Greg Lilly doing the honors on the oars. After lunch, though, I switched to a big white-wool sculpin.

"Good choice," Lilly said in his usual quiet voice that never betrays how hard he's working. "You won't move as many fish with that streamer as with a Girdle Bug, but every fish you see will be bigger."

And so they were.

Streamers in
Still Water

7

Parmachene Lake sits in a small bowl amid the low hills of western
Maine, hidden in a wilderness of private timberland where the
people are vastly outnumbered by deer and moose. Henry Wells explored and fished this country in the late nineteenth century and im-
mortalized its fishing in such books as *Fly Rods and Fly Tackle.* His
gaudy Parmachene Belle wet fly is famous the world over as a brook-
trout classic.

Above the lake in the Magalloway flowages is Cleveland Eddy, a
favorite spot of the late president's where big trout and landlocked
salmon rest in a large river bend after chasing smelt or preoccupied
with their own spawning runs and reluctant to take a fly. This area was
a favorite of Eisenhower's, also, and the old Brown Paper Company
worked hard at milking the publicity generated by their famous guest.
The old fishing logs show some excellent catches, even after World
War II when the late Jack Atherton took a six-pound salmon from the
lake, but the rambling old Victorian hotel is long gone, eroded first by
time and then by fire. There are still a handful of camps on the lake,
because Boise Cascade honors the old leases while it works the land
for pulp and keeps this wilderness otherwise gated and private. The
privacy is a precious anachronism: a huge tract kept much as it was
100 years ago.

For trout on a streamer fly, the Parmachene water is classic. Many
hold streamers to have been a Maine development in the first place,
Supervisors and Ghosts coming from lakeside benches at Rangeley a
few miles south and east around the turn of the century. I slipped
along in the canoe with no small sense of mission, and beached it
quietly at the outlet flowage. There's an old log-cribbing dam here, a
decaying relic of the log-drive days built long before the rising price of

paper made it less expensive to truck the logs and keep them all instead of running the river and losing some.

"Don't start too close to the dam," Paul Bofinger had warned me. "As it gets dark, the trout and salmon drift down to where the current quickens at the outlet. If you get too close before it starts to get dark, you'll spook them."

So I sat on a rock and waited. The long channel was a slow-moving current, and its bubbles passed by almost imperceptibly until they suddenly quickened and disappeared through the cribwork and into the river. A fish rose quietly against the bank. Then another rise came in the shadows, followed by another. I tied on a small slim Supervisor streamer and dropped it in the water to soak. I finally cast toward the dam and twitched the fly gently as it swung toward the logs. There was a boil and a tug and a brook trout's bulldogging fight, and the fish finally came to the gravel where I sat. A bright fish, perhaps a pound in weight, and I watched it swim slowly over a gravel bar toward the lake after I removed the hook from its jaw.

It was a picture-book evening with both trout and salmon coming readily to small streamer flies. The size of the fish increased as darkness fell, and I finished with a brook trout of almost three pounds. It was also a typical prime location for stillwater trout on streamer flies and served as a reminder of a curious truism about stillwater-trout fishing: The best stillwater fishing is usually where the water isn't still at all.

The inlets and outlets of trout ponds and lakes usually offer fertile and shallow water, home to aquatic plants that shelter insect larvae and small minnows on which trout feed. There is often a deeper channel at both inlet and outlet that's attractive to cruising trout that forage in the currents. Finding such channels and currents and fishing across them are usually the keys to catching trout.

Streamer-fly fishing in lakes is most often done by trolling, which is beyond the scope of this book (See, however, the book *Trolling Flies for Trout and Salmon* by Dick Stewart and Bob Leeman [1982, American Angler]). In the absence of obviously feeding fish, casting and fishing streamers can be an awful lot of work, albeit sometimes productive.

Stream-dwelling trout hold positions in the current that are usually obvious, providing a streamer fisherman with targets over which to

Stan Shepardson with an exceptional brook trout taken while casting his
streamer from a canoe in a north-country pond.

Inlets of major rivers are almost always prime stillwater spots. This is the meeting of the Saranac River and Lake Champlain in New York, where landlocked salmon school in spring to feed on smelt, emerald shiners, and young-of-the-year yellow perch.

work his fly. Stillwater trout, even in likely spots such as inlets, can be almost anywhere, and you'll have to spread your casts over a much greater area to find them. In many stream situations, the trout's strike immediately follows its sighting of the moving fly. In still water, however, a trout may follow a moving streamer for many yards before deciding to strike or turn away.

Both of these attributes require repetitive and very long casts when streamer-fishing still water, and the effort can be exhausting. You can make things easier for yourself with a shooting-head system such as I described in Chapter 2. With either shooting heads or conventional fly lines, you'll want at least two different types: a floating or intermediate, and a fast-sinking version.

The open waters of lakes and ponds are often windy, and this wind creates a series of surface currents that can belly a floating line in disconcerting fashion. Intermediate lines and shooting heads sink very slowly, just slowly enough to get below the surface chop and to allow you to keep a straight line when retrieving your fly. These lines are also slightly smaller in diameter and typically stiffer than a regular floating line of the same designated weight, which allows them to be cast greater distances more easily. On the other hand, the downwind shoreline of a lake is usually a productive spot because the wind concentrates surface food here and trout often seem to like the turbulent chop of the waves in such a spot. In this case, a floating line cast across the wind will belly toward the shoreline. Thus your streamer is drawn in a semicircle past the shoreline instead of straight away from it if you're anchored some distance away, and this can be a very effective tactic.

For much of the season in many lakes and ponds, trout will be concentrated around springs on the bottom or in deeper channels between weed beds. In either case, you'll probably need a sinking line to reach the fish. A fast-sinking shooting head is the most versatile type, so I'll use that as an example. The same shooting head you use for river fishing should work well, and remember to use a relatively short leader to keep the fly at the same depth as the sunken line.

Deeper channels may be obvious just from looking as you cruise around in your boat or canoe. Spring holes are usually less obvious, but in a lake or pond that's fished often you can usually find them either by asking someone or watching where other people fish. Anchor your boat or float tube (yes, I sometimes use a belly-boat anchor to keep from being blown around) in such a way that you can cover the channel or spring with a series of casts. If you don't have specific knowledge of what the fish are feeding on at the time, you'll usually have your best luck using a fly with lots of inherent action, such as a Woolly Bugger or Zonker.

Cast over the channel or hole and wait until you think the line has sunk sufficiently to reach the fish. While you're waiting, you need to do a couple of things. First, get ready for a strike, which means keeping your rod tip low and the line straight between you and the fly. With wiggly flies, especially, a strike can come while the fly is simply sinking. Second, keep track of the time allowed for the line to sink. The method usually prescribed is to "count down" as the line sinks and until you start retrieving. You can do this by methodically count-

Slowly cruising the shoreline and casting a big Muddler connected this angler with a Labrador brookie.

ing, although in this electronic age I sometimes use the stopwatch feature on a digital wristwatch. If a sinking period of twenty seconds doesn't produce a fish or bottom hook-up, try twenty-five seconds on the next cast and so forth until you get one or the other.

Varying your retrieve is always critical, and all the more so in this kind of fishing. The fly's deep movement may attract a trout that comes over simply to investigate. Now you have to convince the unseen fish that your fly is good to eat. So strip and stop. Then strip a couple of times and use a briefer stop. Then strip fast three or four times and stop. And change again. This variation in pace is usually critical in bringing a strike. Eventually, and after catching a number of fish, you'll probably find a retrieve pattern that produces best. This pattern may change from day to day, even by the hour, and from lake to lake, so experimentation is the key.

I broadcast a long series of casts across a still lagoon with a Black Marabou to take this outsize Alaskan rainbow.

Such are the general tactics of streamer-fly fishing in still waters. Like most other methods, catching the most fish is usually a matter of little tricks and nuances picked up along the way. One such involves fishing in relatively shallow ponds where you can *see* fish cruising and feeding. Such ponds are most common in the Rocky Mountain and northwestern regions. They may be discrete ponds or lakes or simply large backwaters of rivers or spring creeks.

In such a case you'll most often be using a floating line and a fairly long leader. Cast your streamer well ahead of and in the anticipated path of a cruising fish, then let the fly sink to the bottom and stay there. As the trout approaches the fly, twitch the fly suddenly from the bottom to resemble a natural startled by the approaching trout. Nine times out of ten, the trout will hit viciously before the fly can escape. This takes iron nerves while waiting for the strike, and not a little luck, since you're trying to predict the fish's cruising path.

You'll find many other such tricks in my own book *Stillwater Trout* (1980, Nick Lyons Books), which is still available as a paperback. And in pointing that out, I have a confession to make. I would rather fish a river than a lake. And in a lake or pond, I'd rather fish with drys or nymphs to feeding fish than to fish blind with streamers, which is much more work. But if I'm not near the fish that I love, I love the fish I'm near. That means fishing still water at least sometimes, and at least sometimes with streamers.

Streamers in Small Streams

8

L ittle trout streams remind me of Victorian novels, full of charm and guile and twisted passages and secrets hidden and revealed. Their appeal is audible, too; a mixture of water sounds sometimes muted, other times roaring over miniature cataracts to almost drown the soft whistling of a nearby thrush. The beauty of such water is made intense by its smallness. For a fisherman, the vastness of woodland or meadow holds no more precious secret than that of a small and secret pool.

They will be sheltered on windy days that blow you off the big river, but the mosquitoes will be thick, too. They may spread and slow near a seeping spring that pulls trout to its coolness and where you may go wader-deep in icy muck. They may punctuate a pasture with deep meanders and willow-lined corners certain to hold trout, about which you can wonder as you gauge the distance between you, the bull, and the gate. They are also difficult to fish well.

Small-stream tactics derive from the problems of trying to catch trout in clear, confined quarters without scaring them first. Streamer flies can be effective in such waters, which I'll discuss as two distinct types. The first is a tumbling woodland stream or brook, characterized by riffles and waterfalls and occasional deeper pools. The second is a meadow meander, which is typically flat water through pastureland characterized by S-shaped curves in the creek channel and usually with deeply undercut banks. And to give some meaning to the term "small," let's assume we're discussing streams less than twenty-five feet wide.

The trout are easier in tumbling brooks where the current's broken surface helps to hide a fisherman's approach. The exception is in the tails of the larger pools, where the largest fish may be found holding in

71

shallow, quiet water. These might be trout measured in pounds, too, for the mere fact of a small stream doesn't always mean small fish, as we'll see.

Streamer-fly fishing upstream is difficult, at best. Even in larger rivers with lots of elbow room, upstream fishing usually means line-stripping at a herculean rate to keep the fly alive as it sweeps toward you in the current. For that reason, I've omitted upstream fishing from this book, including this chapter, even though the upstream method can be best for other fly types on small waters.

Fishing downstream is easier, of course, and its success depends on your being able to manipulate your fly in a lifelike manner near the trout while you remain hidden. If circumstances permit, I fish most rapidly flowing small streams by wading right down the middle. A fast current usually means the bottom is rock and gravel, which means my footsteps aren't churning up clouds of silt that would wash down-stream and spook unseen fish. The important considerations here are in going slowly and in fishing a long-enough line so the fish get an undisturbed look at the fly.

I don't need to cast often when fishing this way, relying instead on my reach with a nine-foot rod from side to side to steer the floating line and shallow-swimming streamer into likely holes and pockets. Be-cause my fly is in the water almost all the time as I work my way slowly down-current, I sometimes get strikes that I hadn't antici-pated—in the grassy shallows, for example, just because my fly is passing through.

Using enough line is the difference between catching fish and get-ting skunked when fishing in this manner, especially since you're ap-proaching inherently spooky fish head-on. I try to use as much line as I can control without getting it hung up on rocks and snags. This may mean fifty or sixty feet of floating line if the channel is fairly straight and free-flowing, or as little as fifteen or twenty feet if I have to guide the fly around large boulders and logs.

The little stream behind my house in Vermont is a tumbling brook that stays cold in summer even though its flow is almost bare-bones by September. For years, it's been the source of small mountain brook trout for my own young worm fishermen. On a summer afternoon after a thunderstorm had brought a rise of murky water, I took a small

Small streams that are rapidly tumbling are best fished straight downstream, using your reach with a long rod to move the fly teasingly from
bank to bank. This is the New Hampshire headwaters of the Connecticut
River.

Clear water in small, rapid streams still permits a downstream approach
to the fish as long as you fish a sufficient length of line to avoid spooking
them.

streamer pattern down to the brook with the intention of getting a
mess of little brookies to run through the smoker.

The first time I trailed the small Black Ghost in a little pool it was
whacked by a brown trout almost a foot long. I was astounded, never
having had a clue that such a fish existed here. Within an hour and
over several hundred yards of stream, I took and released a dozen
browns that ran up to fifteen inches—and no brook trout at all. Retro-
spectively, I should not have been so surprised. The little brook does
feed into a major brown-trout stream, and there was no reason

browns shouldn't have colonized its headwaters. It's also a lesson I'm always forgetting and relearning when a bigger river floods and I'm forced to fish the brooks or not fish at all.

When it comes to wading, meadow streams are another matter. Here the relatively soft bottom and slower current mean the trout will be more easily spooked. Fishing carefully from the bank, often on hands and knees, is the best method, because trout in the often-shallow, clear water tend to be exceptionally wary.

Such meadow water is almost invariably more fertile than a tumbling brook, the gentle gradient helping to protect both the trout's food and the trout from the ravages of runoff and floods. There are many little tributary streams and a few spring creeks in the East and Midwest that fall in this category, including the fertile little chalk streams of northern Wisconsin. The high meadows of the Gibbon in Yellowstone and the little spring creeks around Bozeman, Montana, are some Rocky Mountain examples, and there are similar waters from northern California all the way up through the Olympic Peninsula.

Common to most such water is a series of bends, meanders, and S-curves that produce deeper water at the outside edge of the curve. I fish these downstream when using streamer flies, creeping carefully forward to a point at which the bend is a good long cast away. My first cast drops the fly just above the bend and against the shallow bank. The current will swing the fly around toward the deeper water, and I'll punctuate the drift with a twitch or two. When the fly stops against the deeper bank I'll hold it there for a few twitches, and then feed a couple of feet of slack. The fly will drift back slowly, and I'll twitch it slowly forward again. If nothing happens, I'll retrieve the fly slowly away from what I think is productive water and not pick up for another cast until the fly has come far enough upstream in the hole.

This process is repeated with incrementally longer casts until I've managed to cover the entire bend. This approach has one advantage over fishing upstream in that the fly covers the deep big-fish-holding part of the pool first. Upstream fishing in such water usually means fishing to—and often spooking—smaller fish in the pool's tail before the deeper upstream water can be reached. To fish the next downstream bend, I usually have to walk back upstream and wade across to have the deepest bank on my side of the creek, as required by this

This section of the Madison River's South Fork in Montana represents a typical meadow meander. I'll fish this by casting from my knees at position A down to the deep curve marked B.

method.

I can't overemphasize the importance of a cautious approach when fishing this sort of water. There are some clodhoppers who march blithely upright along the bank while looking for fish and casting occasionally. They catch little, and usually see no more than a few small trout streaking for cover. The bigger fish will already be long departed. On some of these streams that are fished often, you may notice two bankside paths. The first will be well-worn and at the very edge of the bank. The second will be much less used—and less apparent—and will be ten or twelve feet back from the edge. The latter path leads to fish.

Basic Streamer Patterns

9

H ere are a dozen basic streamer and bucktail patterns that will work at one time or another no matter where in the world you might try them on trout. Limiting oneself to a dozen patterns for every conceivable situation is a handicap, of course, and most especially so if you need a specific imitation of an emerald shiner or a threadfin shad, to give two examples that aren't represented here.

The list may surprise some by its omissions. For one, the venerable Mickey Finn is not included, and it's been in almost every pattern book since John Alden Knight popularized the pattern in the late 1930s. But the brighter marabous that I have included serve a similar purpose, and their increased versatility is why I've included them instead.

Commercial availability is another criterion, and all of these patterns can be found in most fly shops and catalogs. Commercial availability also implies that the flies are relatively easy to make, which precludes such effective fly styles as Keith Fulsher's Thunder Creek flies. With each of the following patterns, I've included some pertinent tying and fishing notes. For more detailed instruction and a greater selection of patterns, you may wish to check my recent book, *John Merwin's Fly-Tying Guide* (1989, Stephen Greene Press/Viking).

ARGENTINE BLONDE

Hook: Mustad 34007, sizes 3/0 to 3/1
Thread: 6/0 nylon, color to match upper wing
Tail: Yellow bucktail, two shank-lengths long
Body: Gold Mylar tinsel
Wing: Yellow bucktail extending to rear of tail.

This tying style was popularized by the late Joe Brooks, and it's still an excellent big-fish fly in big water. You'll often find it in the saltwater section of shops and catalogs. Other popular color combinations include all-white with a silver body, and a white tail with a medium-blue wing.

BLACK GHOST

Hook: Mustad 9575, sizes 2 to 12
Thread: Black 6/0 nylon
Tail: Yellow hackle fibers
Body: Black floss or wool
Ribbing: Narrow flat silver tinsel
Wing: Four white saddle hackles
Hackle: Yellow, tied as a beard

This Maine classic was designed by Herb Welch in 1927. Welch was a sometime taxidermist, artist, and fly tier who, along with a number of others, claimed to have originated the concept of streamer flies in the early 1900s. This pattern is sometimes adapted as a bucktail and is also tied with yellow and white marabou instead of hackle. I've found the original to be more effective, and it's often my first choice in northeastern waters, especially for brown trout.

Argentine Blonde

Black Ghost

Blacknose Dace

BLACKNOSE DACE

Hook: Mustad 9575, sizes 2 to 12
Thread: Black 6/0 nylon
Tail: Red wool yarn, tied short
Body: Medium flat silver Mylar tinsel
Wing: White bucktail topped by black bucktail topped by medium-brown bucktail

The version of the late Art Flick's pattern is from his book *Art Flick's New Streamside Guide* (1969, Nick Lyons Books). Flick specified a narrower range of sizes, but I've found the large and small extremes useful. He also specified white polar bear hair and black hair from a black bear, but polar bear isn't available as a tying material anymore. I've found it simpler to use bucktail for the entire wing. In very small sizes, you may be able to make these more easily using fine, straight hair from calf tails sold for this purpose.

EDSON TIGER LIGHT

Hook:	Mustad 9575, sizes 2 to 12
Thread:	Yellow 6/0 nylon
Tag:	Fine flat gold tinsel
Tail:	Yellow hackle fibers
Body:	Yellow chenille
Wing:	Natural brown bucktail dyed yellow
Hackle:	Red, tied as a beard

Another venerable Maine pattern, this was originated by Bill Edson in 1929. There's often some confusion about the winging material. From a yellow bucktail, this wing is made from the medium-brown portion on the back that's been dyed to a yellow tint. The wing is thus yellow-brown with tints of brown and black, a good example of the color blending I described in Chapter 3. The wing should extend no farther than the tail to avoid tangling in the hook bend.

GRAY GHOST

Hook:	Mustad 9575, sizes 2 to 12
Thread:	Black 6/0 nylon
Body:	Golden yellow floss
Ribbing:	Medium flat silver tinsel
Wing:	Four peacock-herl strands under a single long golden-pheasant crest feather, topped by four light gray (dun) saddle hackles
Throat:	Sparse long white bucktail next to body with a short golden-pheasant crest feather underneath
Shoulder:	Silver-pheasant body feathers
Cheeks:	Jungle cock or substitute

This pattern has more than one "authentic" version, as do many famous flies simply because the originator changed the pattern slightly from time to time without altering the principles of its construction. This was true of many Stevens patterns, and especially so of this one. This version comes from the book *Trolling Flies* by Stewart and Leeman, mentioned earlier. Note that the fly in the photo is tied with most of the saddle hackles' length overlying the sides of the body, as per my discussion of this fly in Chapter 3.

Edson Tiger Light

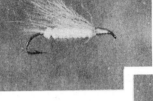

Gray Ghost

Marabou Muddler

MARABOU MUDDLER

Hook: Mustad 38941, sizes 2 to 8
Thread: Light gray 6/0 nylon
Tail: Red hackle fibers
Body: Medium flat silver Mylar tinsel
Wing: White marabou
Topping: Five or six peacock-herl strands
Head: Light tan deer hair spun and clipped Muddler-style with rearward fibers left untrimmed as a collar

These flies are most widely used in the Rockies and West, often with bodies of flashy Mylar tubing instead of tinsel. Black wing/black head is another favorite combination, as is a yellow wing with a gold body. I've often seen brown-winged versions for sale, but I've never had much luck with brown marabou. Another excellent big-trout fly, especially in larger hook sizes. Don't be bashful about using big ones!

BADGER MATUKA

Hook: Mustad 9575, sizes 2 to 12
Thread: Brown 6/0 nylon
Body: Cream dubbing, with a short section of scarlet dubbing right behind the head
Ribbing: Fine oval gold tinsel
Wing: Four badger saddle hackles bound to body Matuka-style with turns of ribbing
Hackle: Badger hackle wound in front of wing and tied back

An old New Zealand streamer style made popular here in the 1970s through the writings of Carl Richards, Doug Swisher, Dave Whitlock, and others. Badger hackle is imitative of many minnows with dark median stripes, and the tying style prevents wing tangling. Often tied in all-black versions and also olive, using olive-dyed grizzly hackles for the wing.

MUDDLER MINNOW

Hook: Mustad 38941, sizes 2 to 14
Thread: Tan 6/0 nylon
Tail: Mottled turkey quill
Body: Medium flat gold Mylar tinsel
Wing: Sparse gray-squirrel tail fibers topped by two sections of mottled turkey quill, tied wet-fly style
Head: Tan deer hair spun and clipped, leaving rearward fibers untrimmed as a collar

Originated by Don Gapen in the late 1930s for Ontario brook trout and popularized about twenty years later by Joe Brooks and Al Mc-Clane through their respective columns in *Outdoor Life* and *Field & Stream*. The late Dan Bailey in Montana gave the fly its present form. A sparse dressing works best in larger sizes. Ultra-small Muddlers are very effective, too, and Fran Betters got me hooked on fishing them around his New York Ausable region. This may be America's most popular fly pattern.

Badger Matuka

Muddler Minnow

Light Spruce

LIGHT SPRUCE

Hook: Mustad 9575, sizes 2 to 12
Thread: Black 6/0 nylon
Tail: Three or four peacock-sword fibers, tied short
Body: Rear half red floss; front half peacock herl
Wing: Four badger saddle hackles
Hackle: Badger wound full and tied slightly back

One of the earliest streamer patterns to emerge from the West and still one of the most widely used. The Dark Spruce is the same pattern except with wings and hackle using dark furnace hackles instead of badger. I've had spectacular fishing for large brown trout on Montana's Big Horn River using the Dark Spruce fished deeply and slowly on frosty October mornings.

WOOLLY BUGGER

Hook: Mustad 79580, sizes 2 to 12
Thread: Black 6/0 nylon
Tail: Black marabou, fairly full and tied shank length; a few fibers Krystal Flash optional
Body: Dark olive chenille
Hackle: Long, soft black saddle hackle palmered forward over body

Originally tied in the East by Russell Blessing, this fly became a standard across the country during the early 1980s. Tied in a variety of colors, this version is the original. It is most specifically imitative of a juvenile bullhead catfish, but its wiggly, enticing action accounts for its success almost anywhere. If I had to pick one fly for big rainbow trout, this would be it.

WOOL SCULPIN

Hook: Mustad 79580, sizes 2 to 8
Thread: Light gray 6/0 nylon
Body: Cream dubbing or wool
Ribbing: Oval silver tinsel
Wing: Strip of cream rabbit fur
Fins: Lightly barred hen hackle feathers
Head: Cream wool, spun and clipped Muddler-style

This pattern is adapted from the excellent *Fly Patterns of Yellowstone* by Craig Mathews and John Juracek (1987, Nick Lyons Books), who described a darker, olive version. This design is one of the most lifelike in the water I've ever seen. It can be tied in a wide variety of colors from light to dark. I like to fish lighter versions near the surface; darker near the bottom. Clumped and trimmed wool can give an excellent head shape and sinks readily, which deer-hair Muddlers do not.

ZONKER

Hook: Mustad 79580, sizes 2 to 8
Thread: Red 6/0 nylon

Woolly Bugger

Wool Sculpin

Zonker

Under-body:	Metallic tape folded over shank and trimmed to give deep belly profile
Body:	Silver Mylar tubing slipped over underbody and tied off at both ends
Wing:	Strip of natural tan rabbit fur tied down with thread at front and rear of body
Hackle:	Natural soft grizzly saddle wound full and tied slightly back

Originated by Dan Byford in Colorado, this is another streamer that became widely popular during the 1980s. Many commercial versions omit the formed underbody and just use Mylar tubing, which makes this wonderfully effective design slightly less effective as the deep-belly flash is lost. Tied in a variety of colors, the rabbit wing offers a terrifically seductive and wavy action in the water.

Bibliography

*There are only three books devoted entirely to streamer fishing, of
which this is one. A few others offer pertinent chapters. Here are a few
of the best.*

BATES, JOSEPH D., Jr. *Streamers and Bucktails.* New York: Knopf,
1979.

BROOKS, JOE. *Trout Fishing.* New York: Outdoor Life/Harper & Row,
1972.

MERWIN, JOHN. *John Merwin's Fly-Tying Guide.* New York: Stephen
Greene Press/Viking, 1989.

MERWIN, JOHN. (ed.) *Stillwater Trout.* New York: Lyons & Burford,
1980.

SCHWIEBERT, ERNEST. *Trout.* New York: E. P. Dutton, 1978.

STEWART, RICHARD and BOB LEEMAN. *Trolling Flies for Trout and
Salmon.* American Angler, North Conway, NH: 1982.